It's amazing what people do with quotations. Agatha Christie murdered them, Bertie Wooster mangled them, Margaret Thatcher and Ronald Reagan spout them and Nigel Rees collects them . . .

In this third book based on his popular radio programmes he has gathered together an entertaining pot-pourri of verbal lore including many marvellous quotes you won't find in any ordinary dictionary or anthology of quotations.

"Quote . . . Unquote" 3 pays special attention to Anon (that prolific minter of quotable quotes), sentiments that could have been better expressed in graveyards, unbelievable but real book titles, and household names that accompany some rather less than household faces.

'If I had a quote,' Bob Dylan once said, 'I'd be wearing it'. The good quotes are here. Try them for size.

"Quote... Unquote" 3

Nigel Rees

London
UNWIN PAPERBACKS
Boston   Sydney

First published in Great Britain by George Allen & Unwin 1983
First published by Unwin Paperbacks 1985

UNWIN ® PAPERBACKS
40 Museum Street, London WC1A 1LU, UK

Unwin Paperbacks
Park Lane, Hemel Hempstead, Herts HP2 4TE, UK

George Allen & Unwin Australia Pty Ltd
8 Napier Street, North Sydney, NSW 2060, Australia

Unwin Paperbacks with the
Port Nicholson Press
PO Box 11–838 Wellington, New Zealand

© Nigel Rees Productions Ltd 1983, 1985

ISBN 0-04-827142 X

Paperback edition based on the hardback designed
by David Pocknell's Company

Illustrated by Michael ffolkes and others.

Printed in Great Britain
by Guernsey Press Co. Ltd
Guernsey, Channel Islands

Contents

'He wrapped himself in quotations – as a beggar would enfold himself in the purple of emperors.'

Rudyard Kipling, The Finest Story in the World

Preface

I think it was George Bernard Shaw who said 'Only fools preface Prefaces with quotations.'

In fact, I *know* it *wasn't* George Bernard Shaw. I am merely following the custom adopted by so many who are called upon to speak or write. The names Oscar Wilde, Winston Churchill and Orson Welles may be substituted for Shaw, but the form remains the same.

Notice particularly the use of 'I think'. This is inserted to give the speaker the air of a man who is familiar with everything worth quoting but does not wish to appear too effortlessly knowledgeable. In all probability the speaker had no idea that Shaw, Wilde, Churchill or Welles ever said any such thing until, shortly before standing up to speak, he opened a dictionary of quotations. No matter. He decided to start with a quotation to lend his theme dignity and himself a whiff of erudition. The choice of Shaw is instructive, however. He is an OK name to quote. So much so that even if G.B.S. never uttered anything remotely similar you can get away with quoting remarks he never made.

Hence, *Rees's First Law of Quotation*: 'When in doubt, ascribe all quotations to George Bernard Shaw.'

The law's first qualification is: 'Except when they obviously derive from Shakespeare, the Bible or Kipling.' The first corollary is: 'In time, all humorous remarks will be ascribed to Shaw whether he said them or not.'

Why should this be? People are notoriously lax about quoting and attributing marks correctly, as witness an analogous process I shall call *Churchillian Drift*.

The *Drift* is almost indistinguishable from the *First Law*, but there is a subtle difference. Whereas quotations with an apothegmatic feel are normally ascribed to Shaw, those with a more grandiose or belligerent tone are, as if by osmosis, credited to Churchill. All quotations in translation, on the other hand, should be attributed to Goethe (with 'I think' obligatory).

Shaw, Churchill, Wilde and Welles are, in fact, fixed in the popular mind as practically the sole source of witty and quotable sayings. Quite how Orson Welles found his way into this pantheon, I'm not so sure – perhaps because of his Falstaffian stature. But what is alarming is the way in which almost any remark not obviously tied to some other originator will one day find itself attributed to one of these four.

In the first edition of the second volume in the 'Quote . . . Unquote' series Orson Welles took unto himself a remark uttered in reality by Billy Wilder. Earlier, an item in the first volume had given rise to an example of pseudo-*Churchillian Drift* which did not actually involve any of the Big Four. I included a remark I had noted down after seeing a performance of Alan Bennett's play *Forty Years On*. I emphasise 'noted down' because it does not occur in the play's printed text: 'Sidney and Beatrice Webb – two nice people if ever there was one.' Imagine my amusement when I came across this line in someone else's anthology attributed to *Arnold* Bennett.

Clearly, the second anthologist either misread his own handwriting or he was afflicted by an attack of

Churchillian Drift.
'Somehow', he must have thought to himself, 'this unfamiliar line needs to be ascribed to someone rather more venerable (and more dead) than Alan Bennett. What could be more appropriate than to donate it to Arnold Bennett – a contemporary of Shaw and Churchill?'

Having written this, I am only too aware that I am open to *Rees's Second Law of Quotation*: 'However sure you are that you have attributed a quotation correctly, an earlier source will be pointed out to you.' For example, in the first

'Quote . . . Unquote' book I stated that Somerset Maugham took the title of his story *Cakes and Ale* from Shakespeare's Twelfth Night. In no time at all, I received a letter from a reader pointing out that the phrase occurs in a papyrus dated *c.* 1,000 – 900 BC: 'Grant ye cakes and ale and oxen and feathered fowl to Osiris.' I was duly mortified – but I have a suspicion that Somerset Maugham did not know either.

Even when a quotation has become firmly linked with a particular source, there is always someone to put you right about it. In

'*Quote . . . Unquote*' I included Churchill's description of Clement Attlee as 'a sheep in sheep's clothing.' Later I discovered that Churchill himself subsequently detached the remark from Attlee and applied it to Ramsay MacDonald (rather more to the point).

Then along came another phrase-detective who asserted that even if Churchill had uttered either of these sentiments at one time or another, he had been talking unto himself a phrase originated by J. B. Morton, alias 'Beachcomber'. Without re-reading the whole of Beachcomber – a pleasant enough task – I am unable to say if this is so. But it seems quite feasible, even if it is more a case of *Churchillian Grab* than *Churchillian Drift*.

It stands to reason that when a *bon mot* is first uttered, a lot depends on the hearing and memory of those present – or the truthfulness and accuracy of the man who disseminates his own *bon mots*. Yet even when a remark is broadcast widely on radio or television or printed in newspapers and magazines error is likely to creep in.

In fact, strictly speaking, I ought to append to every quotation in this book a covering note of deliberate and vague periphrasis: 'I am not saying it *was* Shaw/ Wilde/ Welles who said this. I am merely suggesting that sources would support the view that thingummy is one of a number of possible options as to who might have been associated with the above remark at one time or another.'

Despite the perils implicit in compiling this kind of anthology, I must make clear my debt to those who allegedly spoke or wrote what it contains. In particular, I am grateful to the Estate of P. G. Wodehouse and the Hutchinson Publishing Group for permission to reproduce extracts from the Jeeves books and to the Editor of the *Telegraph Sunday Magazine* for allowing me to quote from one of my own articles which first appeared there.

I am equally indebted to

those lovers of quotations who helped draw much of the content of this book to my attention. It is based largely on the sixth and seventh series of the BBC Radio 4 programme *Quote . . . Unquote*. Alan Nixon agreeably produced the programmes and they included the wit and wisdom of the following participants:

Douglas Adams, Larry Adler, Alan Bennett, Edward Blishen, Bernard Bresslaw, David Buck, John Byrne, Charles Causley, Peter Cook, Jilly Cooper, Jill Craigie, Russell Davies, Frank Delaney, Judi Dench, Ronald Fletcher, Anne Lorne Gillies, Robert Gittings, Brian Glover, Celia Haddon, Cliff Hanley, Russell Harty, Edna Healey, Susan Hill, Martin Jarvis, P. D. James, Brian Johnston, Peter Jones, P. J. Kavanagh, Irma Kurtz, Robert Lacey, John Lahr, Rula Lenska, Naomi Lewis, Henry Livings, Isabelle Lucas, Sue MacGregor, Mary Malcolm, Arthur Marshall, Brian Matthew, Christopher Matthew, Julian Mitchell, John Mortimer QC, Spike Mullins, Derek Parker, Molly Parkin, Peter Porter, Jimmy Reid, Fiona Richmond, Kenneth Robinson, Gay Search, Ned Sherrin, Rosemary Anne Sisson, Janet Suzman, Paul Theroux, Leslie Thomas, Joan Turner, Wynford Vaughan-Thomas, Dick Vosburgh, Sir Huw Wheldon, Kenneth Williams, Terry Wogan.

Thousands of radio listeners also contributed. To them I am most grateful. In the wonderful words from Rutland Boughton's opera *The Immortal Hour*:

'They laugh and are glad . . . and are <u>terrible</u>!'

11

If You Haven't Got Anything Nice To Say About Anyone, Come And Sit By Me

These words were embroidered on a cushion at the Washington DC home (nicknamed 'Detached Malevolence') of Alice Roosevelt Longworth. The daughter of President Theodore Roosevelt, she died aged 96 in 1980 after a lifetime spent making caustic remarks about American political figures. 'Just a slob' was how she described President Harding; 'a poor boob', Eisenhower. 'One-third sap, two-thirds Eleanor' was Alice's comment on her cousin Franklin. The two barbs for which she is most famous, she admitted picking up from others: Calvin Coolidge 'looked as if he had been weaned on a pickle'. 'The Man on the Wedding Cake' helped destroy Thomas E. Dewey, who stood against Truman.

No cushion is needed to provoke the following pointed remarks, even if their recipients might wish they had been cushioned against them.

Pushing forty? She's clinging on to it for dear life.

Ivy Compton-Burnett

Butter wouldn't melt in her mouth. Or anywhere else.

Elsa Lanchester

She looked like Lady Chatterley above the waist and the gamekeeper below.

Cyril Connolly on Vita Sackville-West, who tended to dress in twinset and pearls with gaiters

12

You'll never get on in politics, my dear, with *that* hair.

> *Nancy Astor to a young*
> *Shirley Williams*

I married beneath me. All women do.

> *Nancy Astor on William*
> *Waldorf Astor*

I cannot bring myself to vote for a woman who has been voice-trained to speak to me as though my dog has just died.

> *Keith Waterhouse on*
> *Margaret Thatcher, 1979*

Little Day you've had a busy man.

> *Bud Flanagan on Florence*
> *Day, the actress and variety*
> *artiste*

Looks and sounds not unlike Hitler – but without the charm.

> *Gore Vidal on William F.*
> *Buckley Jnr*

Being attacked by Sir Geoffrey Howe is like being savaged by a dead sheep.

> *Denis Healey, Chancellor of*
> *the Exchequer, 1978*

Not as nice as he looks.

> *Winston Churchill on Ian*
> *Mikardo*

Come again when you can't stay so long.

> *Walter Sickert at the end of a visit from Denton Welch*

He is remembered chiefly as the Prime Minister about whom all is forgotten.

> *Nicolas Bentley on Henry Campbell-Bannerman*

It's probably a case of when the mouse is away, the cats will play.

> *Winston Churchill on Clement Attlee's reluctance as Prime Minister to fly to Moscow*

But, Willie, how sad. If I'd known he was in town, I'd have asked you to bring him.

> *Emerald Cunard to Somerset Maugham, who had told her he was dieting to keep his youth*

Harold Wilson (1964): Why do I emphasise the importance of the Royal Navy?
Heckler: Because you're in Chatham.

Reporter: It is said that you are the best thing the [Australian] Labor Party has going for it. What would happen if you fell under a bus tomorrow?
Gough Whitlam: With the improvements my government has initiated in urban transport, this is unlikely to happen.

From the Sydney Morning Herald, *9 October 1975:*

OPPOSITION CHIEF WOP!

The session [in the Australian House of Representatives] began when a Government backbencher, Dr R. T. Gun, objected to the Opposition Whip, Mr J. W. Bourchier, calling for a quorum during a debate on defence estimates. Dr Gun called out: 'Why don't you shut up, you great poofter.' Mr Bourchier responded: 'Come around here, you little wop, and I will fix you up.'

Tat!

> Calvin Coolidge to a woman who was trying to persuade him that women were every bit as able as men and said: 'Why, Mr President, I can give you tit for tat any time.'

Oh yes, and who *were* you?

> Lord Berners to woman who, when complaining of the bad service on a sea cruise, had said: 'You know, they didn't seem to know who we were.'

He looks like the painting in Wedgwood Benn's attic.

> *William Rushton on Richard Ingrams*

DEDICATED GRATEFULLY TO THE WARDEN AND FELLOWS OF ST ANTONY'S COLLEGE, OXFORD – EXCEPT ONE.

> *Jan Morris*, The Oxford Book of Oxford

The Characters And Incidents Portrayed . . .

'. . . and the names used herein are fictitious and any similarity to the names, character or history of any person is entirely accidental and unintentional' – so runs the somewhat superfluous disclaimer at the start of the film *One Million Years BC*. The dialogue of that film consisted entirely of grunts. Can you supply the titles of the films these rather more literate lines come from.

The answers are on page 20.

1
'Chapter One. He adored New York City. He idolised it out of all proportion.'

2
Prove to me that you're no fool
Walk across my swimming pool.

3
I *am* big. It's the *pictures* that got small.

4
Yes, I killed him. And I'm glad, I tell you. Glad, glad, glad.

5
Randy! Where's the rest of me?

6
The calla lilies are in bloom again.

7
Do you just do your writing now – or are you still working?

8

Come with me to the Casbah.

9

Like Webster's Dictionary, we're Morocco-bound.

10

And did the earth move for you?

11

Yeah, well, that's the way it crumbles, cookie-wise.

12

[Me] Tarzan – [You] Jane!

13

There are eight million stories in *** ***** ****. This has been one of them.

14

Would you be shocked if I put on something more comfortable?

15

'Tain't a fit night out for man nor beast.

16

It's showtime, folks!

17

All my pupils are the *creme de la creme*. Give me a girl of an impressionable age, and she is mine for life.

18

A man's gotta do what a man's gotta do.

Answers
The Characters And Incidents Portrayed . . .

1

Manhattan (1979)   The opening words of the film as Isaac Davis (Woody Allen) tries to begin a novel.

2

Jesus Christ Superstar (1973)   Herod to Christ in the film based on the stage musical (book and lyrics by Tim Rice).

3

Sunset Boulevard (1950)   Gloria Swanson as Norma Desmond, relic of the silent cinema.

4

The Letter (1940)   Bette Davis says it.

5

King's Row (1941)   Ronald Reagan has his legs amputated by a vengeful surgeon and wakes up to utter this deathless line. He used it as the title of his autobiography.

6

Stage Door (1937)   A line beloved of Katherine Hepburn impersonators. It comes from a play within the film.

7

Charlie Bubbles (1968)   Joe Gladwin as a waiter says it to the author (Albert Finney), who replies: 'No . . . I just do the writing.'

8

Trick question. It is a line forever associated with Charles Boyer and *Algiers (1938)* but is not in the film.

9

The Road to Morocco (1942)   Bob Hope and Bing Crosby sing it.

10

For Whom the Bell Tolls (1943)   Gary Cooper after a passionate night with Ingrid Bergman. In the Ernest Hemingway novel, the line appears as: 'But did thee feel the earth move?' (She replies 'Yes'.)

11

The Apartment (1960)   Shirley MacLaine says to Jack Lemmon: 'Why can't I ever fall in love with somebody nice like you?' He makes this reply. She in turn uses the phrase to Fred MacMurray.

12

Tarzan the Ape Man (1932)   This was how the line was delivered in the first sound Tarzan film (without the 'me' and 'you'). Script (amazingly) by Ivor Novello.

13

The Naked City (1948)   A phrase also used in a later TV series.

14

Hell's Angels (1930)   Jean Harlow says it to Ben Lyon. Often quoted as 'Excuse me while I slip into something more comfortable.'

15

The Fatal Glass of Beer (1932)   W. C. Fields says it.

16

All That Jazz (1980)   The opening words of the film, spoken by Roy Scheider.

17

The Prime of Miss Jean Brodie (1969)   The last words of the film, spoken by Maggie Smith.

18

Shane (1953)   Spoken by Alan Ladd.

On Your Quotation Marks!

A notice on the dedication page of Howard Spring's first novel, *Shabby Tiger*, published in 1934, states: 'The author of this novel and all the characters mentioned in it are completely fictitious. There is no such city as Manchester.' Which is an example of starting a novel even before the first line. The following are the first words of novels and plays, or of real people who have just done something momentous. Do you recognise them?

The answers are on page 26.

1

Merde!

2

In a hole in the ground there lived a ******.

3

I have a very important message for the Duke of Hamilton.

4

Ever since childhood, when I lived within earshot of the Boston and Maine, I have seldom heard a train go by and not wished I was on it.

5

I knew I would like her when I saw how her backside moved under her red satin skirt.

6

******, light of my life, fire of my loins. My sin, my soul.

7

All happy families resemble one another, every unhappy family is unhappy after its own fashion.

8

I wish either my father or my mother, or indeed both of them, as they were in duty equally bound to it, had minded what they were about when they begot me.

9

'Take my camel, dear,' said my Aunt Dot, as she climbed down from this animal on her return from High Mass.

10

It was the afternoon of my eighty-first birthday, and I was in bed with my catamite when Ali announced that the archbishop had come to see me.

11
I shall not say why and how I became, at the age of fifteen, the mistress of the Earl of Craven.

12
Everywhere the glint of gold.

24

13

Don't worry, it's quite suitable for the children. This is a story about passion, bloodshed, desire and death – everything in fact that makes life worth living.

14

Of late years an abundant shower of curates has fallen upon the North of England.

15

A Saturday afternoon in November was approaching the time of twilight and the vast tract of unenclosed land known as ***** ***** enbrowned itself moment by moment.

16

Did you hear what I was playing, Lane?

17

I have been here before.

18

Ours is essentially a tragic age, so we refuse to take it tragically.

19

It was about eleven o'clock in the morning, mid-October, with the sun not shining and a look of hard wet rain in the clearness of the foothills.

20

I will sit down now, but the time will come when you will hear me.

Answers
On Your Quotation Marks!

1

The play *Ubu Roi* by Alfred Jarry.

2

(Hobbit) J. R. R. Tolkien, *The Hobbit*.

3

Preceded by the words 'Yes, I am German. I am Hauptman Alfred Horn. I want to go to Dungavel House.' This is what Rudolph Hess, once Hitler's deputy, said when he parachuted into Scotland in May 1941. He had a peace plan with him and asked to see the Duke of Hamilton, whom he had met at the Berlin Olympics five years earlier.

4

Paul Theroux, *The Great Railway Bazaar*.

5

James Hadley Chase, *No Orchids for Miss Blandish*.

6

(Lolita)   Vladimir Nabokov, *Lolita*.

7

Tolstoy, *Anna Karenina*.

8

Laurence Sterne, *Tristram Shandy*.

9

Rose Macaulay, *The Towers of Trebizond*.

10

Anthony Burgess, *Earthly Powers*.

11
Harriette Wilson, *Memoirs* (the ones which gave rise to the Duke of Wellington's 'Publish and be damned!')

12
Howard Carter, recalling his first sight inside the tomb of Tutankhamun.

13
The stage musical *Irma-La-Douce* (adapted in the film version).

14
Charlotte Brontë, *Shirley.*

15
(Egdon Heath)   Thomas Hardy, *The Return of the Native.*

16
Oscar Wilde, *The Importance of Being Earnest*. (Algernon Moncrieff to Lane, his manservant, who replies 'I didn't think it polite to listen.')

17
Evelyn Waugh, *Brideshead Revisited* – first words of Chapter 1, but there is a Prologue.

18
D. H. Lawrence, *Lady Chatterley's Lover.*

19
Raymond Chandler, *The Big Sleep.*

20
Benjamin Disraeli, during his less than successful maiden speech in the House of Commons, 12 December 1837.

If I Had A Good Quote, I'd Be Wearing It

After an alfresco performance in Paris, Bob Dylan was shivering in the night air when a French reporter came up and asked him for a 'good quote'. Replied Dylan: 'If I had a good quote, I'd be wearing it.'

Try these on for size.

Your cameraman might enjoy himself because my face looks like a wedding-cake left out in the rain.

W. H. Auden, to a reporter

My good fellow, why not carry a watch?

Sir Herbert Beerbohm Tree, to a man struggling under a grandfather clock

The British churchman goes to church as he goes to the bathroom – with the minimum of fuss and no explanation if he can help it.

> *Ronald Blythe*

Whatever 'in love' means.

> *Prince Charles, February 1981, on his engagement to Lady Diana Spencer, when asked if he was 'in love'. She answered 'Of course.'*

The smile of a woman who has just dined off her husband.

> *Laurence Durrell, on the* Mona Lisa

I'm sorry, ladies and gentlemen, I would like to land but there's a gentleman here who would prefer to go to Le Touquet in France.

> *Captain Eddie Foley on an Aer Lingus flight to Heathrow, faced with a failed Trappist monk hijacker, May 1981*

Ladies and gentlemen, this is your captain speaking. We have a small problem. All four engines have stopped. We are doing our damnedest to get them working again. I trust you are not in too much distress.

> *Captain Eric Moody of British Airways as his 747 ran into a volcanic storm over southern Sumatra and plunged 25,000 feet before his crew managed to get the engines restarted, July 1982*

After you've met one hundred and fifty Lord Mayors, they all begin to look the same.

King George V

Q.   Is it your intention to overthrow the Government of the United States by force?
A.   Sole purpose of visit.

Gilbert Harding, filling in immigration form

The Prince of Wales' brother, along with some other,
Slaps me on the back and says, 'Come and see mother.'
I'm Bert, Bert, and Royalty's hurt, when they ask me to dine,
    I say, 'No–,
I've just had a banana with Lady Diana,
I'm Burlington Bertie from Bow.'

William Hargreaves, writer and composer of Burlington Bertie from Bow, *1915*

Mr Mencken has just entered a trappist monastery in Kentucky and left strict instructions that no mail was to be forwarded. The enclosed is returned, therefore, for your archives.

H. L. Mencken's standard rejection slip when editor of the American Mercury

The people of Zaire are not thieves. It merely happens that they move things, or borrow them.

President Mobutu of Zaire, 1978

Shooing them on sight.

> *Dr Mahathir bin Mohamed, deputy Prime Minister of Malaysia, claiming that this is what his forces would be doing if the Vietnamese boat people tried to land, in June 1979 – not 'shooting them on sight'.*

I am not going to rearrange the furniture on the deck of the *Titanic*.

> *Rogers Morton, declining to make any bold moves to salvage President Ford's ailing campaign for re-election, 1976*

I have had my [TV] aerials removed. It's the moral equivalent of a prostate operation.

> *Malcolm Muggeridge, 1981*

I have been sensible far too long, and now I need not be sensible, at least for the time being.

> *William Rees-Mogg, on relinquishing editorship of* The Times *and becoming Deputy Chairman of the BBC*

I have a face like the behind of an elephant.

> *Charles Laughton*

If you subtracted the North Sea oil revenues, you would realise that present policies are leading us to the status of a banana republic that has run out of bananas.

Sir Richard Marsh, 1978

Bloody hell, Ma'am, what's he doing in here?

> *Chambermaid Elizabeth*
> *Andrews's reaction to the*
> *intruder in the Queen's*
> *Buckingham Palace*
> *bedroom, July 1982*

It often happens that I wake at night and begin to think about a serious problem and decide I must tell the Pope about it. Then I wake up completely and remember that I *am* the Pope.

> *Pope John XXIII*

Thank God the sun has gone in. I shall not have to go out and enjoy it.

> *Logan Pearsall Smith*

When asked his opinion of Welsh nationalism, Mr Thomas replied in three words, two of which were 'Welsh nationalism'.

> *newspaper report about*
> *Dylan Thomas*

No, no! Jimmy Stewart for Governor, Reagan for best friend.

> *Jack Warner, when told that*
> *Ronald Reagan wanted to*
> *run for Governor of*
> *California*

If they played my favourite tune, everyone would have to stand up.

John Wayne

He is going round the country stirring up apathy.

William Whitelaw on Harold Wilson, 1975

Nobody we know, dear.

Coral Browne to companion, when an enormous phallus was revealed as the centrepiece of the National Theatre's set for a production of Oedipus, *1968*

It's Not Mecca, It Just Smells Like It

Neil Simon's characterisation of New York in *California Suite* brings us to some notable quotations about cities, counties, and countries. Fill in the blanks from the choices listed. The answers are on page 38.

1

When _____ sneezes, Europe catches cold.
VIENNA, BERLIN, PARIS

2

For _____ people rarely smile
Being urban, squat, and packed with guile.
DURHAM, CAMBRIDGE, OXFORD

3

When I am lying awake at night, and the pale moonlight streams through the latticed casement, strange fancies crowd upon my poor mad brain, and I sometimes think that if we could hit upon some word for you to use whenever I am about to relapse – some word that teams with hidden meaning – like _____ – it might recall me to my saner self.
CHIPPING SODBURY, GODALMING, BASINGSTOKE

4

_____ is a geographical expression.
SWITZERLAND, LAS MALVINAS, ITALY

5

_____, where the nuts come from.
IRELAND, POLAND, BRAZIL

6
O _____! stern and wild
Meet nurse for a poetic child
Land of brown heath and shaggy wood,
Land of the mountain and the flood.
MACEDONIA, CALEDONIA, ESTONIA

7
_____ is the Mother of Parliaments.
ENGLAND, WESTMINSTER, ICELAND

8
An acre in _____ is better than a principality in Utopia.
MIDLOTHIAN, MIDDLESEX, MANCHESTER

,,

Answers
It's Not Mecca, It Just Smells Like It

1
PARIS – according to Metternich, 1830.

2
CAMBRIDGE – in Rupert Brooke's poem
The Old Vicarage, Grantchester.

3
BASINGSTOKE – from the opera *Ruddigore*, words by
Sir W. S. Gilbert.

4
ITALY – Metternich again, in 1849.

5
BRAZIL – as in 'I'm Charley's Aunt from Brazil, where the
nuts come from' – *Charley's Aunt*, the play by
Brandon Thomas.

6
CALEDONIA (the Roman name for Scotland) –
in Sir Walter Scott's *The Lay of the Last Minstrel.*

7
ENGLAND – John Bright, 1865.

8
MIDDLESEX – Macaulay, 1837.

Men And Horses I Have Known

In the library at Blenheim Palace, I once spotted a book with the title *Men and Horses I Have Known*. I felt sure that the book could not live up to such a superb title and so I did not attempt to read it. I suspect the same is true of these other intriguing tomes. They have all been given to books which actually exist (if only at the Frankfurt Book Fair, where each year a special watch is kept out for improbable titles).

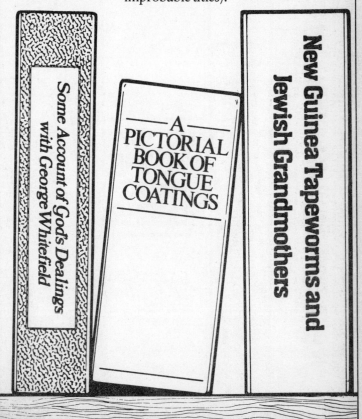

Some Account of God's Dealings with George Whitefield

— A —
PICTORIAL
BOOK OF
TONGUE
COATINGS

New Guinea Tapeworms and Jewish Grandmothers

CHILD-SPACING IN TROPICAL AFRICA

The Biochemist's Songbook

Last Chance at Love: Terminal Romance

SHORT TERM VISUAL
INFORMATION FORGETTING

The
ROMANCE
of
LEPROSY

The Sex Life of Robinson Crusoe

Cooking with God

Buddhism in fifteen minutes

The Interpretation of Geological Time
from the Evidence of Fossilised
Elephant Droppings in Eastern Europe.

Agatha Christie Did It

It's no wonder, in the light of the previous section, if authors, instead of inventing their own book titles, steal them. Agatha Christie did it quite regularly. Her most famous play, *The Mousetrap*, owed its name to the play-within-a-play in *Hamlet*:

King Claudius: What do you call the play?
Hamlet: 'The Mouse-trap' . . . 'tis a knavish piece of work: but what of that?

Where did Dame Agatha find these other titles? The answers for this entire section are on page 50.

1

The Mirror Crack'd

Murder Most Foul

Taken at the Flood

Other authors resort to very obscure sources for their titles.
James Hilton's 1941 novel *Random Harvest* (later filmed)
sprang from an error in German wartime propaganda
when 'the Hun' claimed to have attacked the town of
'Random', following a British communiqué to the effect that
'bombs were dropped at random'.

Mary Hayley Bell thought that her title *Whistle Down the
Wind* was original until Len Deighton pointed out to her
that it occurs in Shakespeare as 'I'd whistle her off and
let her down the wind' (a hawking metaphor from
Othello, III. iii).

R. F. Delderfield had a way of giving his books titles which sounded like quotations but which defy tracing to source. *A Horseman Riding By* sounds as if it ought to be a quotation, as does *To Serve Them All My Days*. Probably the latter contains no more than echoes of several religious lines: 'And to serve him truly all the days of my life' from the Catechism in *The Book of Common Prayer*; 'To serve thee all my happy days', from the hymn 'Gentle Jesus, meek and mild' in the Methodist Hymnal; the Devon carol

'We'll bring him hearts that love him
To serve him all our days';
and the Sunday school hymn
'I must like a Christian
Shun all evil ways,
Keep the faith of Jesus,
And serve him all my days.'

These novelists appear to have had no qualms about borrowing direct. Where from? Answers on page 50.

6
Simon Raven: Places Where They Sing

7
Emma Lathen: Double, Double, Oil and Trouble

8
James Baldwin: The Fire Next Time

9
Iris Murdoch: An Unofficial Rose

10
Robert Penn Warren: World Enough and Time

11
Evelyn Waugh: Put out more Flags

12
P. D. James: Cover Her Face

I say, you fellows

And, lastly, the sources of the titles borrowed for the following biographies, autobiographies and other works of non-fiction:

26
Dean Acheson: Present at the Creation

27
Evelyn Waugh: A Chapter of Accidents

28
Douglas Jay: Change and Fortune

29
Sheilah Graham: Scratch an Actor

30
Stewart Grainger: Sparks Fly Upward

31
Howard Thomas: With an Independent Air

32
Antonia Fraser: Cromwell: Our Chief of Men

33
David Niven: The Moon's a Balloon

34
Malcolm Muggeridge: Tread Softly for you Tread on my Jokes

35
What two books by Gay Talese take their titles from Exodus 20?

Answers
Agatha Christie Did It

1

Tennyson, *The Lady of Shalott*: 'Out flew the web and floated wide/The mirror crack'd from side to side'.

2

Shakespeare, *Hamlet*, I.v. This was the title of a Miss Marple film although it was based on a Hercule Poirot novel called *Mrs McGinty's Dead* – which, as far as I know, is not from *Hamlet*.

3

The Catechism in *The Book of Common Prayer*: 'Question: What is your name? Answer: N or M.' N is for *nomen* (name) and M is in place of NN for *nomina* (names).

4

Shakespeare, *Sonnets*, 98: 'From you have I been absent in the Spring'.

5

Shakespeare, *Julius Caesar*, IV.iii: 'There is a tide in the affairs of men/Which, taken at the flood, leads on to fortune.' Curiously, the title of the novel in the US was *There is a Tide*.

6

The Rubric after the Third Collect in *The Book of Common Prayer*: 'In Quires and Places where they sing, here followeth the Anthem.'

7

Shakespeare, *Macbeth*, IV.i: 'Double, double toil and trouble'.

8

'That prophecy re-created from the Bible in a song by a slave – God gave Noah the rainbow sign,/No more water, the fire next time.'

9

Rupert Brooke, *The Old Vicarage, Grantchester*: 'Unkempt about those hedges blows/An unofficial English rose.'

10

Andrew Marvell, *To His Coy Mistress*: 'Had we but world enough, and time/This coyness, lady, were no crime.'

11

Chinese sage: 'A drunk military man should order gallons and put out more flags in order to increase his military splendour.'

12

John Webster, *The Duchess of Malfi*, IV.ii: 'Cover her face; mine eyes dazzle: she died young.'

13

T. S. Eliot, *Whispers of Immortality*: 'Webster was much possessed by death/And saw the skull beneath the skin.'

14

The phrase occurs in Dryden and Shakespeare but Sherriff's autobiography reveals no more than that he took it from 'It was late in the evening when we came at last to our Journey's End' in a book he does not name.

15

From the nursery rhyme *Little Boy Blue*: 'Little boy blue,/Come blow your horn,/The sheep's in the meadow,/The cow's in the corn.'

16

From the nursery rhyme *A Frog He Would A-Wooing Go*:
'Pray, Mrs Mouse, are you within?/Heigh ho! says Rowley.'

17

The Naval Discipline Act 1860: 'Conduct unbecoming the
character of an officer.'

18

W. E. Henley, *To W.R.*: 'Madame, Life's a piece in bloom,
Death goes dogging everywhere:
She's the tenant of the room,
He's the ruffian on the stair.'

19

From the song *Bless 'em All* or, more probably, its parody
Sod 'em All: 'Sod 'em all. Sod 'em all,
The long and the short and the tall.'

20

W. H. Auden, *Birthday Poem*
(sometimes called *August for the People*):
'August for the people and their favourite islands.'

21

A. E. Housman, *A Shropshire Lad*:
'What are those blue remembered hills,
What spires, what farms are those?'

22

John Braham, *The Americans*: 'England, home and beauty.'

23

Song of Solomon 2:10: 'Take us the foxes, the little foxes,
that spoil the vines.'

24

Tennyson, *Idylls of the King*:
'For why is all around us here
As if some lesser God had made the world,
But had not force to shape it as he would?'

25

Song of Solomon 2:12: 'The voice of the turtle is heard in
our land.'

26

Alfonso the Wise, King of Castile: 'Had I been present at the
Creation, I would have given some useful hints for the better
ordering of the universe.' (On studying the Ptolemaic system.)

27

Fourth Earl of Chesterfield: 'A chapter of accidents', 1753;
John Wilkes: 'The chapter of accidents is the longest chapter
in the book' (quoted 1837).

28

A. E. Housman, *Last Poems*:
'When summer's end is nighing
And skies at evening cloud,
I muse on change and fortune
And all the feats I vowed
When I was young and proud.'

29

Dorothy Parker: 'Scratch an actor and you'll find an actress.'

30

Job 5:7: 'Man is born unto trouble, as the sparks fly upwards.'

31

From the song *The Man Who Broke the Bank at Monte
Carlo*: 'As I walk along the Bois Bou-long
With an independent air'.

32

Milton, Sonnet 16, 'To the Lord General Cromwell':
'Cromwell, our chief of men, who through a cloud,
Not of war only, but detractions rude,
Guided by faith and matchless fortitude,
To peace and truth thy glorious way had ploughed.'

33

e. e. cummings, *& N &*: 'Who knows if the moon's a
balloon, coming out of a keen city
in the sky – filled with pretty people?'

34

W. B. Yeats, *He Wishes for the Cloths of Heaven*:
'I have spread my dreams under your feet;
Tread softly, for you tread on my dreams.'

35

Honour Thy Father; Thy Neighbour's Wife. The first was
about the mafia, the second was a study of sexual *mores* in
the US. Talese also wrote a book about the *New York Times*
and called it *The Kingdom and the Power*, another of those
titles which sounds like a quotation but isn't.

We Do People Things

During his interesting researches for the book *Thy Neighbour's Wife*, Gay Talese spent a good deal of time with a colony called Sandstone, which grew out of a nude encounter group in Los Angeles. Meeting one of the women for the first time, he asked 'But what do you people in these nude groups do?' Said she 'We do people things.'

That is one way of putting it. Here are some others:

Cannes is where you lie on the beach and stare at the stars – or vice versa.

Rex Reed, film critic

I struggled for forty-seven years. I distinguished myself in every way I possibly could. I never had a compliment, nor a 'Thank you', nor a single farthing. I translated a doubtful book in my old age, and I immediately made sixteen thousand guineas. Now that I know the tastes of England, we need never be without money.

Sir Richard Burton, translator of the first unexpurgated edition of The Thousand and One Nights

I tend to believe that cricket is the greatest thing that God ever created on earth . . . certainly greater than sex, although sex isn't too bad either. But everyone knows which comes first when it's a question of cricket or sex – all discerning people recognise that. Anyway, don't forget one doesn't have to do two things at the same time. You can either have sex before cricket or after cricket – the fundamental fact is that cricket must be there at the centre of things.

Harold Pinter

I was sitting near two elderly colonial types in a restaurant during the great period of 'butter' jokes following the opening of *Last Tango in Paris* in 1973. The man admitted having seen the film and the woman pressed him to explain the fuss about the butter. 'Well, they got very excited about the butter,' he explained diplomatically. 'But why?' she pressed on. 'Did he *throw* it at her?'

You've made a happy man feel very old.

> *Terry-Thomas in* The Last
> Remake of Beau Geste

There's a lot of promiscuity about these days and I'm all for it.

> *Ben Travers, aged 94, 1980*

A. You are the greatest lover I have ever known.
B. Well, I practise a lot when I'm on my own.

> *Woody Allen*, Love and
> Death

Masturbation is the thinking man's television.

> *Christopher Hampton*, The
> Philanthropist

[We] are really the Liz Taylor and Richard Burton of the seventies.

> *Britt Ekland on her liaison
> with Rod Stewart, 1977*

I say I don't sleep with married men, but what I mean is that I don't sleep with happily married men.

Britt Ekland, 1980

You mean, apart from my own?

Zsa Zsa Gabor, in reply to the question 'How many husbands have you had?'

Tell me about yourself – your struggles, your dreams, your telephone number.

Peter Arno

Lord Castlerosse was taken to task by Nancy Astor over the size of his stomach. 'What would you say if that was on a woman?' she asked, pointedly. 'Half-an-hour ago it was,' he replied.

Splendid couple – slept with both of them.

Sir Maurice Bowra, when asked what he thought of the happy pair at an Oxford wedding

Somerset Maugham asked Winston Churchill if he had ever had any homosexual experience. 'Once', said Churchill, 'I went to bed with a man to see what it was like.' 'Who was it?' probed Maugham. 'Ivor Novello,' replied Churchill improbably. 'And what was it like?' asked Maugham. 'Musical. . . .'

In Joe Orton's play *The Ruffian on the Stair*, the hero describes what is obviously a homosexual experience. An outraged Irishman exclaims: 'There is no word in the English language for what you've been doing!' The retort is: 'In Lapland they have no word for snow.'

Never eat at a place called Mom's. Never play cards with a man called Doc. Never go to bed with a woman whose troubles are greater than your own.

Nelson Algren

I'll come and make love to you at five o'clock. If I'm late, start without me.

Tallulah Bankhead

A*L*P*H*A*B*E*T* S*O*U*P

So many new agencies were set up under Franklin D. Roosevelt's New Deal, most of which came to be known by their initials, that Al Smith said the government was 'submerged in alphabet soup'. The trouble with acronyms and groups of initials generally is that they are open to more than one interpretation. First, though, what are these acronyms *supposed* to mean? The answers are on page 64.

1
WASP

2
TIR (as on the backs of lorries)

3
UNCLE (as in 'The Man from . . .')

4
M*A*S*H*

5
INRI

6
SOS

7
NATSOPA

8
NIBMAR

9
GI

10
ERNIE

11
ENSA

12
WRVS

13
QANTAS (yes, it is an acronym)

14
CREEP (or CRP, originally)

Inevitably, different interpretations of some of these initials were soon to hand. ENSA became 'Every Night Something Awful' or 'Even Naafi Stands Aghast'. The WRVS, before it acquired royal patronage, was said to stand for 'Widows, Virgins and Spinsters'. The BBC's Head of CAMP (Current Affairs Magazine Programmes) has not attracted further translation.

The decorations CMG, KCMG, and GCMG (respectively Companion, Knight Commander and Knight Grand Cross of the Order of St Michael and St George) have traditionally been interpreted as 'Call Me God', 'Kindly Call Me God' and 'God Calls Me God'.

People are even keen to detect an acronym where there isn't one. Down Under, Hestin bras are said to 'Hold Every Size of Tit In (Australia)'.

Then there are initials devised informally to cover various social and sexual matters. The word 'posh' is said to be derived from 'Port Out, Starboard Home' – indicating the most sought-after cabins when travelling to and from the Orient by boat. Smart businessmen travelling the Atlantic came up with the variant COSH – 'Concorde Out, Skytrain Home'. Others include:

BURMA Be Upstairs/Undressed Ready, My Angel
CIBP Comb In Back Pocket
FHB Family Hold Back (when hospitality is in danger of running out)
ITALY I Trust/Treasure And Love You
NORWICH (K)Nickers Off Ready When I Come Home
N(Q)OCD Not (Quite) Our Class, Dear
NQTD Not Quite Top Drawer
NST Not Safe in Taxis
PITP Pen In Top Pocket
PLU People Like Us
POETS Piss Off Early, Tomorrow's Saturday
TGIF Thank God It's Friday
VPL Visible Panty Line
WHT Wandering Hand Trouble

Before the 1948 nationalisation of railways in Britain, the initials of the private companies gave rise to inventive interpretations:

GWR (Great Western Railway) God's Wonderful Railway; Great Way Round; Go When Ready
LMS (London, Midland & Scottish) Hell of a Mess; Let Me Sleep; The Lord's My Shepherd
LNER (London & North Eastern) Late and Never Early Railway
MGN (Midland & Great Northern) The Muddle and Go Nowhere
MSL (Manchester, Sheffield & Lincolnshire) The Muck, Sludge and Lightning
S & D (Somerset & Dorset) Slow and Dirty
SE & C (South Eastern & Chatham) The Slow, Easy and Comfortable

Nowadays, the same spirit demands that airline names be subjected to the same treatment:

ALITALIA Always Late In Take-off, Always Late In Arrival; Aircraft Landing In Tokyo, All Luggage In Australia
BOAC Better On A Camel; Bend Over Again, Christine
El Al Everything Lousy, Always Late
LUFTHANSA Let Us F*** The Hostesses And Not Say Anything
PAL Pick Another Line
PAN AM Pilots Are Normally All Maniacs
QANTAS Queer And Nasty, Try Another Service
SABENA Such A Bloody Experience, Never Again
TAP Take Another Plane
TWA Try Walking Across

Answers
A*L*P*H*A*B*E*T* S*O*U*P

1
White Anglo-Saxon Protestant

2
Transports Internationaux Routiers

3
United Network Command for Law and Enforcement

4
Mobile Army Surgical Hospital

5
Iesus Nazarenus, Rex Iudaeorum (Jesus of Nazareth, the King of the Jews – according to St John's gospel only, the title which was fixed to the cross by order of Pontius Pilate).

6
(The three dots and three dashes and three dots do *not* stand for 'Save Our Souls' or 'Save Our Ship' – they were chosen merely for ease of transmission and recognition.)

7
National Society for Operative Printers and Assistants

8
No Independence Before Majority Rule

9
General Issue *or* Government Issue

10
Electronic Random Number Indicator Equipment

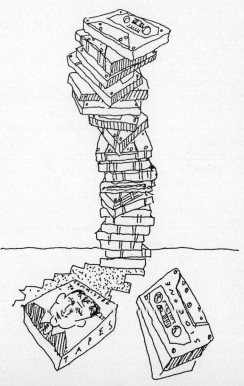

Hullo, Fathead . . . What News On The Rialto?

Unusually, this is Bertie Wooster's Aunt Dahlia plucking a line from Shakespeare in *Aunts Aren't Gentlemen* by P. G. Wodehouse. Usually, it is Bertie who is fumbling for the apt quotation and, more often than not, believing that Jeeves invented all the best lines. When Jeeves quotes 'It is a far, far better thing', Bertie comments 'As I said before, there is nobody who puts these things more neatly than he does'. A quotation from Shakespeare is frequently accompanied by 'As I have heard Jeeves put it' or 'To quote one of Jeeves's gags'. For example, 'Leaving not a wrack behind, as I remember Jeeves saying once.'

Although we are told that Jeeves is quite capable of reading Spinoza's *Ethics*, such trust in his ability to coin a neat phrase is strange in a Wooster educated at Eton and Oxford and winner of the Scripture Knowledge prize. As Richard Usborne has pointed out, Bertie's frame of reference is no more than one would expect of an educated man in the early twentieth century. There are curious lapses, though: 'The next moment I was dropping like the gentle dew upon the place beneath. Or is it rain? Jeeves would know.' Occasionally, Bertie resorts – as so many of us do – to 'as the fellow said'. In one book he refers to 'the works of somebody called Wordsworth.'

Some quotations recur throughout the Jeeves canon. 'With a wild surmise' probably crops up most often. Bertie worries obsessively and understandably over 'the cat i' the adage' and 'fretful porpentine'. What is more, Wodehouse lards these novels with more literary allusions as he grows older. *Jeeves in the Offing*, published in 1960, contains forty-eight.

It is a delight when Bertie alludes to 'Shakespeare and those poet Johnnies' by way of attribution or when he scrambles his quotations, as in 'One man's caviar is another man's major-general, as the old saw has it.' But help him out with these. What quotations is he groping for? The answers are on page 73.

1

Right from the first day he came to me, I have looked on [Jeeves] as a sort of guide, philosopher, and friend.

The Inimitable Jeeves

2

[Jeeves], do you recall telling me once about someone who told somebody he could tell him something which would make him think a bit? Knitted socks and porcupines entered into it, I remember.

Jeeves in the Offing

3

The snail's on the wing and the lark's on the thorn, or rather the other way round, as I've sometimes heard you say.

Much Obliged, Jeeves

4

Folding the girl in my arms, I got home on her right eyebrow. It wasn't one of my best, I will admit, but it was a kiss within the meaning of the act.

Thank You, Jeeves

5

They were all taking it extremely big. Pop Bassett, like the chap in the poem which I had to write out fifty times at school for introducing a white mouse into the English Literature hour, was plainly feeling like some watcher of the skies when a new planet swims into his ken, while Aunt Dahlia and Constable Oates resembled respectively stout Cortez staring at the Pacific and all his men looking at each other with a wild surmise, silent upon a peak in Darien.

The Code of the Woosters

6

It was nice to feel that I had got my bedroom to myself for a few minutes, but against that you had to put the fact that I was in what is known as durance vile and not likely to get out of it.

The Code of the Woosters

7

'Is it morning?' I inquired.
'Yes, sir.'
'Are you sure? It seems very dark outside.'
'There is a fog, sir. If you will recollect, we are now in autumn – season of mists and mellow fruitfulness.'
'Season of what?'
'Mists, sir, and mellow fruitfulness.'
'Oh? Yes. Yes, I see. Well, be that as it may get me one of those bracers of yours, will you?'

The Code of the Woosters

8

'So this letter stirred you up, did it?'

'You bet it stirred me up,' she said. 'I felt I couldn't wait another day without seeing him. What was that poem about a woman wailing for her demon lover?'

'Ah, there you have me,' I said. 'Jeeves would know.'

Thank You, Jeeves

9

'Oh? Well, let me tell you that the man that hath no music in himself . . .' I stepped to the door. 'Jeeves,' I called down the passage, 'What was it Shakespeare said the man who hadn't music in himself was fit for?'

'Treasons, stratagems, and spoils, sir.'

'Thank you, Jeeves.'

Thank You, Jeeves

69

10

'We shall meet at Philippi, Jeeves.'

'Yes, sir.'

'Or am I thinking of some other spot?'

'No, sir, Philippi is correct.'

'Very good, Jeeves.'

'Very good, sir.'

Thank You, Jeeves

11

'But what can I say about the sunset?' asked Gussie.

'Well, Jeeves got off a good one the other day. I met him airing the dog in the park one evening, and he said, "Now fades the glimmering landscape on the sight, sir, and all the air a solemn stillness holds." You might use that.'

Right Ho, Jeeves

12

He greets you as if you were a favourite son, starts agitating the cocktail shaker before you know where you are, slips a couple into you with a merry laugh, claps you on the back, tells you a dialect story about two Irishmen named Pat and Mike, and, in a word, makes life one grand, sweet song.

Thank You, Jeeves

13

Cows were mooing in the distance, sheep and birds respectively bleating and tootling, and from somewhere near at hand there came the report of a gun . . . Totleigh Towers might be a place where Man was vile, but undoubtedly every prospect pleased.

The Code of the Woosters

14

I don't know if you were ever told as a kid that story about the fellow whose dog chewed up the priceless manuscript of the book he was writing. The blow-out, if you remember, was that he gave the animal a pained look and said: 'Oh, Diamond, Diamond, you – or it may have been thou – little know – or possibly knowest – what you – or thou – has – or hast – done.' I heard it in the nursery, and it has always lingered in my mind.

The Code of the Woosters

15

I remember Jeeves saying to me once, apropos of how you can never tell what the weather's going to do, that full many a glorious morning had he seen flatter the mountain tops with sovereign eye and then turn into a rather nasty afternoon.

The Code of the Woosters

16

'Jeeves,' I said, 'As I have often had occasion to say before, you stand alone.'

'Thank you, sir.'

'Others abide our question. Thou art free.'

'I endeavour to give satisfaction, sir.'

Thank You, Jeeves

17

That is the problem which is torturing me, Jeeves. I can't make up my mind. You remember that fellow you've mentioned to me once or twice, who let something wait upon something? You know who I mean – the cat chap.

The Code of the Woosters

"

Answers
Hullo, Fathead . . . What News On The Rialto?

1

Pope, *An Essay on Man*: 'Shall then this verse to future age pretend/Thou wert my guide, philosopher, and friend?'

2

'I think you may be referring to the ghost of the father of Hamlet, Prince of Denmark, sir. Addressing his son, he said, "I could a tale unfold whose lightest word would harrow up thy soul, freeze thy young blood, make thy two eyes, like stars, start from their spheres, thy knotted and combined locks to part and each particular hair to stand on end like quills upon the fretful porpentine." '

3

Browning, *Pippa Passes*: 'The lark's on the wing;/The snail's on the thorn.'

4

Betting Act: 'A place within the meaning of the Act'.

5

Keats, *On First Looking into Chapman's Homer*.

6

Burns, *The Epistle from Esopus to Maria*: 'In durance vile here must I wake and weep,/And all my frowzy couch in sorrow steep.'

7

Keats, *Ode to Autumn*.

8

Coleridge, *Kubla Khan*: 'A savage place! as holy and enchanted/As e'er beneath a waning moon was haunted/By woman wailing for her demon-lover.'

9

Shakespeare, *The Merchant of Venice*, V.i.

10

Shakespeare, *Julius Caesar*, IV.iii: 'I will see thee at Philippi' (Brutus to Caesar's ghost).

11

Gray, *Elegy in a Country Churchyard*.

12

Charles Kingsley, *A Farewell. To C.E.G.*: 'And so make Life, and Death, and that For Ever,/One grand sweet song.'

13

Bishop Heber, *From Greenland's Icy Mountains*: 'Every prospect pleases and only man is vile.'

14

Isaac Newton is supposed to have said 'Oh Diamond, Diamond, thou little knowest the mischief thou hast done' when his dog overturned a lighted candle and destroyed the manuscript Newton had laboured many years to complete.

15

Shakespeare, *Sonnets*, 33: 'Kissing with golden face the meadows green/Gilding pale streams with heavenly alchemy.'

16

Matthew Arnold, *Shakespeare*: 'Others abide our question. Thou art free/We ask and ask: Thou smilest and art still/ Out-topping knowledge.'

17

'Macbeth, sir, a character in a play of that name by William Shakespeare. He was described as letting "I dare not" wait upon "I would" like the poor cat i' th' adage.'

There's No More Exhilarating Feeling Than Quoting Winston Churchill

It would be hard to think of a notable phrase introduced by either of those ideologically linked politicians Margaret Thatcher and Ronald Reagan, though each, like Bertie Wooster, appears curiously aware of other people's notable remarks. In his inaugural speech in 1981 President Reagan quoted or alluded to Winston Churchill, John F. Kennedy and even Jimmy Carter, without providing any jewelled epigrams of his own. In March 1981, when the attempt was made on his life, Reagan produced a series of gags and quotes from his hospital bed, evoking the shade of W. C. Fields ('On the whole I'd rather be in Philadelphia'), Churchill ('There's no more exhilarating feeling than being shot at without result'), and Jack Dempsey, the boxer. After losing the world heavyweight championship to Gene Tunney in 1926, Dempsey said to his wife: 'Honey, I forgot to duck.' Reagan, the former sports commentator, said the

same to his wife, Nancy. Addressing both Houses of Parliament in June 1982, Reagan went in for verbal saturation bombing by quoting Churchill half a dozen times.

Margaret Thatcher has managed to keep up. In her 1979 election campaign she indicated how things were going by quoting Kipling: 'Out of some long, bad dream that makes her mutter and moan,/Suddenly, all men rise to the noise of fetters breaking.' When a newspaperman queried the source, it was duly reported that the Prime-Minister-to-be recalled his request in the small hours of the morning and took the trouble to write him a note. In her final pre-election broadcast she rounded off with an unattributed chunk of Noël Coward ('One day this country of ours which we love so much will find dignity and greatness and peace again'). In Downing Street on the day of her victory she quoted Airey Neave ('There is work to be done') and the rather more resonant words of St Francis of Assisi: 'Where there is discord may we bring harmony, where there is error may we bring truth, where there is doubt may we bring faith, and where there is despair may we bring hope.'

It was subsequently revealed that this last quotation had been supplied at four o'clock in the morning by Ronald Millar, the playwright, who shares Mrs Thatcher's literary tastes. When he dashed off a speech for her which included the quote from Abraham Lincoln 'Don't make the rich poorer, make the poor richer', she delved into her handbag and found a piece of yellowing paper on which was written the same Lincoln quotation. She added: 'I take it everywhere with me.'

Since her election, the world has been regaled with snatches of Sir Francis Drake in paraphrase ('When we endeavour any great matter it is not the beginning of the matter but the continuing of the same until it is thoroughly finished that yields great joy'), an extract from the song 'Love and Marriage' relating to trade unions, and, when relieved that her son Mark had not been lost in the Sahara, a line from the genuinely anonymous poet who said 'Life owes me nothing;/One clear morn/Is boon enough for being born.'

At the start of the war in the Falklands, 1982, Mrs Thatcher evoked the spirit of Queen Victoria with a reference to her remark at the end of 'Black Week' in 1899: 'We are not interested in the possibilities of defeat; they do not exist.'

Why do politicians quote so much? With the American President it might be an old actor's inclination to stick to well tried scripts rather than utter anything original. With Mrs Thatcher it is presumably a reflection of a well-stocked mind that seeks to evoke emotions in knee-jerk response to certain emotional triggers.

The short answer must be, however, that politicians are incapable these days of producing memorable phrases themselves – they must get support from others. Politicians' phrases which do catch on are those that can be given in evidence against them and those that are gaffes.

Present-day events seldom provide opportunities for the likes of a Gettysburg address from a modern-day Lincoln, or a 'Blood, toil, tears and sweat' speech from a Churchill. Neither the times nor the men seem capable of giving rise to the mighty line. One reason for this state of affairs must be that politicians seldom write the words they speak. They are too often the mouthpieces for committees of speechwriters. Ronald Millar was awarded a knighthood for coming up with cringeworthy phrases like 'U-turn if you want to, the lady is not for turning' and 'the autumn of understanding' looking forward to a 'winter of common sense'. One wonders if Mrs Thatcher would have done better writing her own speeches.

The rise of radio and television has had a great impact on political speech. Politicians once made formal orations from public platforms (I suppose the House of Commons still provides something of this), but now they temper their thoughts and style to the casual, conversational exchanges of the radio or television studio. Besides, the exposure to which the modern political leader is subjected by the media is much greater than on the public platforms of the old days. The more he says, the less memorable it is.

There is nothing inherently wrong with a politician's urge to quote others. It appears that Mrs Thatcher's recourse to Queen Victoria came about because of a visit to the underground war rooms in Whitehall, where she saw the motto put there by Churchill. But Churchill not only quoted – he was quotable himself. Even Mrs Thatcher's most valued tag of 'Iron Lady' was supplied for her by the Soviet paper *Red Star*. There should surely be a limit to the amount of off-the-peg *réclame* that any politician can produce. Never mind if Edward Kennedy did not write his own speech at the Democratic convention in 1980. At least he managed to come up with the resonant words 'For all those whose cares have been our concern, the work goes on, the cause endures, the hope still lives, and the dream shall never die.'

Still, politicians and others continue to be inclined to quotation. What are the sources of the following examples – some accurate, some not, and some intentionally scrambled? The answers are on page 84.

1

They asked him how he felt after an unsuccessful election. He said he felt like a little boy who had stubbed his toe in the dark. He said that he was too old to cry, but it hurt too much to laugh.

> *Adlai Stevenson, conceding*
> *the 1952 election to Eisenhower*

2

Quiet calm deliberation disentangles every knot.

*a motto chosen by Harold
Macmillan for his private
office and the Cabinet Room
at 10 Downing Street*

3

One can always count on Gilbert and Sullivan for a rousing finale, full of words and music, signifying nothing.

Tom Lehrer

4

'My very noble and approved good masters,' my colleagues, my friends, my fellow students in the great wealth, the great firmament of your nation's generosities, this particular choice may perhaps be found by future generations as a trifle eccentric but the mere fact of it, the prodigal, pure, human kindness of it must be seen as a beautiful star in that firmament which shines upon me at this moment, dazzling me a little, but filling me with warmth and the extraordinary elation, the euphoria that happens at the first breath of the majestic glow of the new tomorrow. From the top of this moment, in the solace, in the kindly emotion that is charging my soul and my heart this moment, I thank you for this great gift which lends me such a splendid part in this your glorious occasion.

*Laurence Olivier accepting
his special Oscar in
Hollywood, 1979*

5

The bad ended unhappily, the good unluckily. That is what tragedy means.

Tom Stoppard, Rosencrantz
and Guildenstern are Dead

6

Under the spreading chestnut tree
I sold you and you sold me:
There lie they, and here lie we
Under the spreading chestnut tree.

George Orwell, Nineteen
Eighty-Four

7

So what we are watching here is a clear case of Mann's
inhumanity to Mann.

*John Arlott, commentating
on a cricket match in which a
South African googly bowler
named 'Tufty' Mann was
tying a Middlesex batsman
called George Mann in knots*

8

A short, sharp shock.

*Recipe for the treatment of
young offenders called for by
William Whitelaw and other
Home Secretaries over the years*

9

Actresses will occur in the best regulated families.

Oliver Herford

10

[Wordsworth] found in stones the sermons he had already
hidden there.

Oscar Wilde

11

If I should die, think only this of me –
That in some corner of a foreign field
There lies a plagiarist.

Derek Alder

12

None but the brave can live without the fair.

Frank McKinney Hubbard

13

I come from haunts of coot and hern.

*woman in Thurber cartoon,
arriving at party brandishing
wild flowers*

14

Life wasn't meant to be easy.

*Malcolm Fraser, Prime
Minister of Australia*

15

He nothing common did or mean
Upon that memorable scene.

*Winston Churchill to Edward
VIII on the day of his
abdication*

16

Sail on, O Ship of State!
Sail on, O Union, strong and great!

*Franklin D. Roosevelt in
letter to Winston Churchill,
January 1941*

17

And not by eastern windows only,
When daylight comes, comes in the light,
In front, the sun climbs slow, how slowly,
But westward, look, the land is bright.

*Winston Churchill, in
broadcast reply to the
foregoing, May 1941*

18

You have sat too long here for any good you have been
doing. Depart, I say, and let us have done with you. In the
name of God, go.

*L. S. Amery to Neville
Chamberlain, House of
Commons, May 1940*

Answers
There's No More Exhilarating Feeling Than Quoting Winston Churchill

1
Abraham Lincoln

2
Sullivan, *The Gondoliers*

3
Shakespeare, *Macbeth*, V.v: '[Life] is a tale/Told by an idiot, full of sound and fury,/Signifying nothing.'

4
Shakespeare, *Othello*, I.iii: 'Most potent, grave, and reverend signiors,/My very noble and approv'd good masters'.

5
Wilde, *The Importance of Being Earnest*: (Miss Prism) 'The good ended happily, and the bad unhappily, that is what Fiction means.'

6
Popular song 'The Chestnut Tree' based on Longfellow, *The Village Blacksmith*: 'Underneath the spreading chestnut tree/The village smithy stands.'

7
Robert Burns, *Man was Made to Mourn*.

8
Sullivan, *The Mikado*: 'To sit in solemn silence in a dull, dark dock,/In a pestilential prison, with a life long lock,/Awaiting the sensation of a short, sharp shock,/From a cheap and chippy chopper on a big black block.'

9
Charles Dickens, *David Copperfield*: (Mr Micawber)
'Accidents will occur in the best-regulated families.'

10
Shakespeare, *As You Like It*, II.i: 'Sweet are the uses of
adversity . . . this our life, exempt from public haunt,/Finds
tongues in trees, books in the running brooks,/Sermons in
stones and good in everything.'

11
Rupert Brooke, *The Soldier*: 'That there's some corner of a
foreign field/That is forever England.'

12
Dryden, *Alexander's Feast*: 'None but the brave deserves the
fair.'

13
Tennyson, *The Brook*: 'I come from haunts of coot and
hern,/I make a sudden sally/And sparkle out among the
fern/To bicker down the valley.'

14
Shaw, *Back to Methuselah*: 'Life is not meant to be easy, my
child; but take courage: it can be delightful.'

15
Andrew Marvell, *Upon Cromwell's Return from Ireland*.

16
Longfellow, *The Building of the Ship*.

17
Arthur Hugh Clough, *Say Not the Struggle Naught
Availeth*.

18
Oliver Cromwell, addressing the Rump Parliament, 1653.

Anon Said It

Squelches, put-downs, personal remarks whose origins are lost in the mists of time. Any information on who uttered them first would be welcome. Meanwhile, they must be credited to the prolific Anon.

Hostess to garrulous guest: 'While you've got your mouth open, would you ask the maid to serve dinner?'

After leaving Johannesburg on a flight to London, a rather smug and self-opinionated woman travelling in the first-class section beckoned the stewardess to come to her. 'Tell me,' she said, 'what's the domestic situation in England these days?' Replied the stewardess: 'I don't think you will have any trouble finding a job, madam.'

Chops were served for the midday meal in hospital and the patients regarded this as quite a treat. Several patients only had the use of one arm, however, and hesitated over how to deal with the chops. 'Use your fingers!' advised one, helpfully. 'Quite the easiest way to deal with a chop, and I assure you it's done in the best circles.' The patient in the next bed said to her: 'I've been in the best circles, and it isn't.'

A group of students was being shown around a house which one young woman had just moved into. They entered a rather messy room. 'This is my room,' she announced proudly. There was a pause. Then someone asked: 'And where do the deer and the antelope play?'

Following the murder of Lord Lucan's nanny, Sandra Rivett, and the good lord's disappearance, police conducted a routine house-to-house inquiry in Belgravia. When one highly-placed old lady was told of the nanny's death, she said to the police officer: 'Oh dear, what a pity. Nannies are *so* hard to come by these days.'

Anon on W. H. Auden: 'He didn't love God, he just fancied him.'

A Franciscan monk – complete with brown habit, girdle, sandals and beard – was travelling on the London Underground when he encountered a group of bovver boys. One of the boys challenged the monk by saying 'And wot d'you think you're supposed to be?' Replied the Franciscan: 'I think I'm supposed to be polite. What do you think you're supposed to be?'

Wee Georgie Wood, the music hall and variety artist, was in his eighties when one day he hailed a taxi cab and said to the driver: 'British Museum, please!' The driver replied: 'You're taking a bloody chance, aren't you!'

Anon on Ramsay MacDonald: 'He died – as he lived – at sea.'

A barrister who worked as legal adviser to a businessman whom he despised was rung up by the businessman's wife to inform him that her husband had died suddenly. 'The funeral's on Wednesday,' she said. 'Are you coming?' 'No,' said the barrister, 'I believe you.'

Anon on his wife: 'They say a woman should be a cook in the kitchen and a whore in bed. Unfortunately, she is a whore in the kitchen and a cook in bed.'

Advancing upon a noted female journalist at a party, an admirer enthused: 'You're great – you're my pin-up girl. As far as I'm concerned, you are the Woman of the Year.' A fellow journalist inquired sourly: 'Which year?'

Another female columnist was being introduced to a gracious lady at a party. 'She is a very well known columnist,' said the introducer, with enthusiasm. Said the gracious lady, 'Oh really, under what name do you write?'

Anon on Sir Alec Douglas-Home: 'I've seen better-looking faces on pirate flags.'

Anon on a participant in a French poetry recital at Eton: 'Didn't she do well! And how wise not to attempt a French accent.'

Anon emerging from the four-hour version of the film Heaven's Gate *in New York*: 'Do you realise if we'd gone on Concorde, we'd be in Paris by now.'

Anon on available Nordic blonde: 'Ah, I see the Danish open sandwich is with us again.'

An Englishman had spent all evening telling Irish jokes in the pub. Suddenly, a man at the next table leaned over indignantly and said 'Oi! You telling Irish jokes! I think you should know that I'm Irish.' To which the Englishman answered apologetically: 'Oh, I'm terribly sorry, pal! If I'd known I'd have told 'em more slowly.'

Anonymous American diplomat on Brendan Bracken, wartime Minister of Information and close colleague of Winston Churchill: 'You're phoney. Everything about you is phoney. Even your hair, which looks false, is real.'

Anonymous Venetian gentleman: 'Why should I travel when I am already there?'

Anon on Randolph Churchill: 'He should not be allowed out in private.'

Answering the door to two people who introduced themselves by saying 'Good morning, we're Jehovah's Witnesses', the white-bearded man replied 'Good. I'm Jehovah. How are we doing?'

<u>By Their Names Shall Ye Know Them</u>

But not necessarily by their faces. The Marquis de Sade, W. Heath Robinson, Dame Nellie Melba, Miss Belinda Blurb and Charles Lynch could wander down the street unrecognised (and a motley crew they would make), but we still make use of words based on the names they bequeathed to us. I hesitate to describe the people whose pictures follow as household names – it rather depends what sort of household you live in – but, using the verbal clues, try and work out what word it is they have contributed to the language.

The answers are on page 96.

1. 'For wearing east of Suez?'

2. 'Blow up and see me some time'

3. 'Don't let them eat cake'

4. 'A cut above the aristocracy'

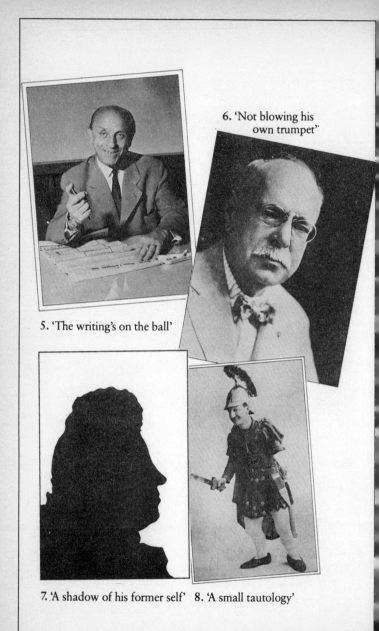

6. 'Not blowing his own trumpet"

5. 'The writing's on the ball'

7. 'A shadow of his former self' 8. 'A small tautology'

9. 'Don't mention Hindenburg'

10. 'Sounds like a panelist'

12. 'Not with a whimper but a bang'

11. 'Dotty character, you see'

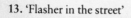
13. 'Flasher in the street'

14. 'Blundering feminist?'

15. 'What a dish down under'   **16.** 'Very cuddly in the bedroom'

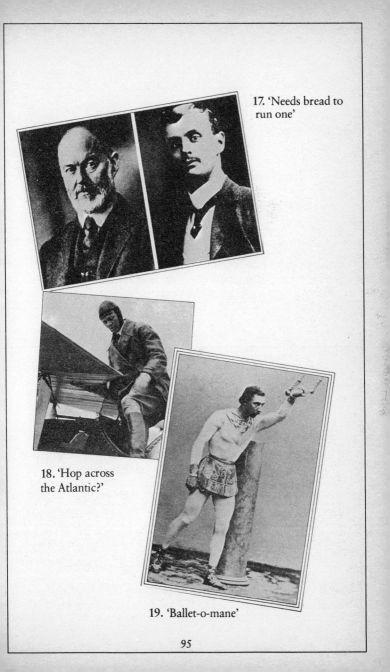

17. 'Needs bread to run one'

18. 'Hop across the Atlantic?'

19. 'Ballet-o-mane'

Answers
By Their Names Shall Ye Know Them

1

ANTHONY EDEN – the popular name for the style of black felt homburg hat worn by Sir Anthony Eden (later Earl of Avon) when Foreign Secretary in the 1930s.

2

MAE WEST – RAF slang for an airman's inflatable life-saving jacket, coined *circa* 1940. Commented the film actress: 'I've been in *Who's Who* and I know what's what but this is the first time I've ever been in a dictionary.'

3

SANDWICH – the 4th Earl of (1718–92), who made his servant bring him slices of meat between pieces of bread so that he could continue gambling without leaving for lunch or dinner.

4

GUILLOTINE – the French physician Joseph-Ignace Guillotin (1738–1814) suggested the 'painless' way of chopping off heads. But he did not invent the machine and was embarrassed when it was called after him.

5

BIRO – Lazlo Biro was a Hungarian artist who emigrated to Argentina where, in 1943, he invented the capillary attraction system which is the basis of ballpoint pens.

6

SOUSAPHONE – John Philip Sousa (1854–1932), the American bandmaster, had the large tuba named after him.

7

SILHOUETTE – Étienne de Silhouette (1709–67) had a brief career as Controller-General in France and gave his name to an equally fleeting kind of portraiture.

8

TICH – Little Tich (1868–1928), the music hall comic, was born Harry Relph but took his stage name from the Tichborne claimant in a famous court case. Now, anybody small is a 'tich'.

9

ZEPPELIN – Count Ferdinand von Zeppelin (1838–1917) was the German designer and manufacturer of airships.

10

QUISLING – Major Vidkun Quisling (1887–1945) was a Norwegian collaborator with the Nazis and gave his name to those who aid occupying forces traitorously.

11

BRAILLE – Louis Braille (1809–52), the French inventor of raised writing for the blind, was himself blind from the age of three.

12

MOLOTOV COCKTAIL – a simple incendiary device, usually a bottle of petrol with a wick, takes its name from V. M. Molotov, the Soviet statesman (born 1890).

13

BELISHA BEACON – Leslie Hore-Belisha was British Minister of Transport (1931–7) and gave his name to the flashing orange globe which indicates a pedestrian crossing.

14
BLOOMERS – Mrs Amelia Jenks Bloomer (1818–94) introduced the Bloomer costume or dress, a style of female dress consisting of a short skirt and long loose trousers gathered closely around the ankles.

15
PAVLOVA – Ballerina Anna Pavlova (1885–1931) is remembered, particularly in Australia, through a meringue cake topped with whipped cream and fruit.

16
TEDDY BEAR – US President Theodore 'Teddy' Roosevelt (in office 1901–9) was noted for his interest in hunting bears but gave his pet name to the children's stuffed variety.

17
ROLLS-ROYCE – The Hon. Charles Stewart Rolls and Frederick Henry Royce developed the motor car and aero engines which bear their joint names.

18
LINDY HOP – a dance craze of the 1930s named after Charles Lindbergh, US aviator, who made the first solo non-stop flight across the Atlantic in 1927.

19
LEOTARD – the tight-fitting covering for ballet dancers and others takes its name from Jules Léotard, the nineteenth-century French acrobat who designed it.

Brief, And To The Point

You know the sort of thing. . . .
'Have struck iceberg. Badly damaged. Rush aid.'
The last SOS from the Titanic.
Crisp, pithy, punchy.
Just like advertising copy.
Or again:
'To hell with you. Offensive letter follows.'
Nice telegram. Alec Douglas-Home once received it.
Shouts, cries, telegrams and cables.
What do they refer to?
The answers are
on page 101.

1
I spy strangers!

2
The Navy's Here!

3
Fourteen hundred!

4
Who goes home?

5
Open, Sesame!

6
Splice the mainbrace!

7
Winston's back!

8
I have gazed upon the face of Agamemnon.

9
Nuts!

10
Heir apparent and his consort assassinated this morning by means of an explosive nature.

"

Answers
Brief, And To The Point

1

In the House of Commons when an MP wishes to draw attention to the presence of strangers with a view to having them excluded. A relic of the days when the proceedings were conducted behind closed doors. In the rare event of it being invoked these days, the public in the galleries and the press have to withdraw at once.

2

In the Second World War, 299 British seamen were rescued from the German ship *Altmark* in a Norwegian fjord. One of the rescuing sailors called out these words and they became famous soon afterwards.

3

The traditional cry in the London Stock Exchange when a stranger ventures on to the trading floor. It dates from the time when the Stock Exchange had 1,399 members.

4

Asked of MPs by doorkeepers at the House of Commons. It dates back to the days when it was necessary for MPs to depart in groups for their own protection from cut-throats and thieves.

5

The password at which the door of the robbers' cave flew open in the Tale of the Forty Thieves in *The Thousand and One Nights*.

6

A naval expression denoting an extra tot of grog all round – possibly from the issue of an extra rum ration to those who performed the difficult task of splicing the mainbrace in the days of sailing ships.

7

A signal sent from the Admiralty to all the ships in the Fleet at the outbreak of the Second World War. Winston Churchill was appointed First Lord – a position he had held at the outbreak of the First World War.

8

Heinrich Schliemann's telegram to the King of Greece, August 1876, on excavating the last grave at Mycenae. Well, he believed it.

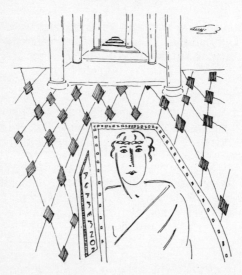

9

American General Anthony McAuliffe replied thus to a German demand for surrender during the Battle of the Bulge in the Second World War.

10

Cable from His Britannic Majesty's Consul in Sarajevo, 28 June 1914.

Or Words To That Effect

During the trial of Jeremy Thorpe on a murder conspiracy charge in 1979 his counsel, George Carman QC, addressed the jury thus: 'I end by saying in the words of the Bible: "Let this prosecution fold up its tent and quietly creep away." '
Unfortunately, we have no redress against misquotation in the High Court of Justice. What's more, Mr Thorpe was acquitted. The quotation Mr Carman was groping for was not from the Bible but from Longfellow's 'The Day is Done':

And the night shall be filled with music
And the cares that infest the day
Shall fold their tents, like the Arabs,
And as silently steal away.

At least the learned QC did not raise a laugh by his error, as did the mayor in the old story who said that during his year of office he felt he had to lay aside all political allegiances and be 'like Caesar's wife, all things to all men'.
Despite the perils implicit in resorting to quotation we all use quotations in everyday speech – sometimes without even knowing we are doing it.
Where do the following well-known phrases originate? Make a choice from the options available. The answers are on page 108.

1
Love me, love my dog.

ST FRANCIS OF ASSISI, J. M. BARRIE, ST BERNARD

2
Bloody but unbowed.

J. M. BARRIE, SHAKESPEARE *(Macbeth)*,
W. E. HENLEY

3
In the country of the blind, the one-eyed man is king.

SAMUEL BUTLER, G. K. CHESTERTON, H. G. WELLS

4
The course of true love never did run smooth.

SHAKESPEARE *(Romeo and Juliet)*, SHAKESPEARE
(A Midsummer Night's Dream), SHAKESPEARE
(Troilus and Cressida)

5
Change and decay in all around I see.

H. F. LYTE, W. E. HENLEY, H. G. WELLS

6
Fools rush in where angels fear to tread.

OLD FRENCH PROVERB, POPE,
SHAKESPEARE *(Richard III)*

7
A policeman's lot is not a happy one.

A. P. HERBERT, DICKENS, W. S. GILBERT

8
To the manner born.

ECCLESIASTES, KIPLING, SHAKESPEARE *(Hamlet)*

9
In the Spring a young man's fancy lightly turns to thoughts
of love.

SHAKESPEARE *(A Midsummer Night's Dream)*,
TENNYSON, BROWNING

10
The glass of fashion, and the mould of form.

CONGREVE, WEBSTER, SHAKESPEARE *(Hamlet)*

11
God moves in a mysterious way.

GRAY, COWPER, SHAKESPEARE *(Hamlet)*

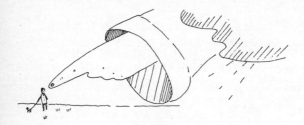

12
Filthy lucre.

KIPLING, ST PAUL'S EPISTLE TO TITUS,
ECCLESIASTES

13
A man more sinned against than sinning.

ST PAUL'S EPISTLE TO TITUS, SHAKESPEARE *(King
Lear)*, SHAKESPEARE *(Othello)*

14
A poor thing but mine own.

SHAKESPEARE *(As You Like It)*, SHAKESPEARE
(Twelfth Night), SHAKESPEARE *(The Tempest)*

15
Screw your courage to the sticking point.

SHAKESPEARE *(Coriolanus)*, SHAKESPEARE
(The Winter's Tale), SHAKESPEARE *(Macbeth)*

16
A plague on both your houses.

SHAKESPEARE *(Macbeth)*, SHAKESPEARE *(King Henry IV, Part 1)*, SHAKESPEARE *(Romeo and Juliet)*

17
Abandon hope, all ye who enter here.

BEFORE THE ORACLE AT DELPHI, AT THE ENTRANCE TO HELL, IN THE COLOSSEUM, ROME

Answers
Or Words To That Effect

1

Curiously enough this occurs over a thousand years ago in the writings of St Bernard. In his first sermon there appears the Latin 'Qui me amat, amet et canem meum.' But just to spoil a good story it was not the St Bernard after whom the dogs are named.

2

W. E. Henley, *Invictus*: 'In the fell clutch of circumstance
I have not winced nor cried aloud
Under the bludgeonings of chance
My head is bloody but unbowed.'

3

H. G. Wells wrote a short story with the title *The Country of the Blind* on this theme but the phrase has proverbial roots (Greek and French). I have also seen the remark attributed to Erasmus.

4

Shakespeare, *A Midsummer Night's Dream*, I.i.

5

H. F. Lyte, in the hymn *Abide with me*.

6

Pope, *An Essay on Criticism*. However, in Shakespeare's *Richard III* there is talk of wrens making prey where eagles dare not perch.

7

W. S. Gilbert, *The Pirates of Penzance*.

8

Shakespeare, *Hamlet*, I.iv: 'Though I am native here
And to the manner born, it is a custom
More honour'd in the breach than the observance.'

9

Tennyson, *Locksley Hall*.

10

Shakespeare, *Hamlet*, III.i.

11

From one of the Olney hymns by William Cowper:
'God moves in a mysterious way
His wonders to perform
He plants his footsteps in the sea
And rides upon the storm.'

12

St Paul's Epistle to Titus 1:11: 'For filthy lucre's sake' (also 1 Timothy 3:3: 'Not greedy of filthy lucre').

13

Shakespeare, *King Lear*, III.ii: 'I am a man
More sinned against than sinning.'

14

A misquotation from Shakespeare's *As You Like It*, V.iv:
A poor virgin, sir, an ill-favoured thing, sir, but mine own.

15

A misquotation from Shakespeare, *Macbeth*, I.vii: 'Screw your courage to the sticking place and we'll not fail.'

16

Shakespeare, *Romeo and Juliet*, III.i:
'A plague o' both your houses
They have made worms' meat of me.'

17

A misquotation of 'All hope abandon, ye who enter here' from the entrance to Hell in Dante's *Inferno*: 'Lasciate ogni speranza voi ch'entrate.'

Titles II

In the beginning there was a book called *'Quote . . . Unquote'*. Now here we are with *'Quote . . . Unquote' 3*. I take comfort from Sylvester Stallone in this tricky titling business. He may have been the first to take a title to the third round by calling his boxing saga *Rocky III*. He chose not to beat about the bush with *Son of Son of Rocky* or *The Return of Rocky* or *Rocky Revisited*, but simply stuck a Roman 'III' after the original title.

In the old days, Hollywood had different ways of being blatant. If the first film had been a success you made sure the public knew it was in for more of the same by harking back to the original with a title like *Son of Kong* (a hasty sequel to *King Kong*), *Son of Monte Cristo*, *Son of Paleface*, *Son of Robin Hood*, *Son of Sinbad*, *Son of Frankenstein*, *Son of*

Dracula and *Son of Ali Baba*. Alternatively, you could stage a comeback with *The Return of Dracula*, *The Return of the Scarlet Pimpernel* and even (quite recently) *The Return of a*

Man Called Horse. The third method was simply to date the pictures: *Gold Diggers of Broadway* was followed by *Gold Diggers of 1933, 1935* and *1937*.

So how was it that numbers became the rage – what with *Jaws 2, The Godfather, Part II* and *French Connection II*? This was a reaction against a peculiar 1960s taste for long-winded titles. For years we had been getting along nicely with mousy little titles like *Ben Hur* and *South Pacific*, when in 1963 we were suddenly confronted with *Dr Strangelove, or How I Learned to Stop Worrying and Love the Bomb*. TV joined in with *That Was The Week That Was* and *Not So Much a Programme, More a Way of Life*. The theatre gave us *Oh Dad, poor Dad, Mama's Hung you in the Closet and I'm Feeling So Sad.*

The world record for a long title is held, I believe, by some sixteenth-century play whose title goes on for about a page. It recounts the plot in so much detail it is hardly necessary to see the play. In the 1960s *The Persecution and Assassination of Marat, as Performed by the Inmates of the Asylum of Charenton under the Direction of the Marquis de Sade* was staged. Anthony Newley, who had previously gone to some lengths with *Stop the World I want to get off* and *The Roar of the Greasepaint, The Smell of the Crowd*, made a film in 1968 with a verbal obstacle course for its title: *Can Hieronymous Merkin ever forget Mercy Humppe (and find True Happiness)?*

One wonders whether they really *wanted* you to go and see films and plays with titles like these. Shows become popular through word-of-mouth recommendation, but if the title is too much of a mouthful, like *It's a Mad, Mad, Mad, Mad World*, it is quite likely you will not talk about it at all. *How to Succeed in Business Without Really Trying* was equally trying and *A Funny Thing Happened on the Way to the Forum* wasn't.

No wonder that towards the end of the 1960s the tide turned towards the simplicity of slapping a numeral after the original title when it came to sequels. The lead had been given by *Time* magazine in September 1939 when it promptly devised the name 'World War II'. In 1969, the Cunard Line's successor to the *Queen Elizabeth* and the *Queen Mary* was not 'The Queen Elizabeth the Second'. It was Queen Elizabeth 2 (not even 'Queen Elizabeth II'), more commonly known as simply 'QE 2'.

Jaws 2 took the hint, as did *Death Wish II*, *Damien: Omen II*, *Friday the Thirteenth, Part II* and several more. There were exceptions of course. The sequel to *American Graffiti* was obviously *More American Graffiti*. Forswearing 'Pink Panther 2', '3' and '4', Blake Edwards gave us *The Pink Panther Strikes Again*, *The Revenge of the Pink Panther*, and *The Return of the Pink Panther*. (I suppose 'Son of the Pink Panther' would have been plain silly.) The 'Airport' films have followed their own peculiar sequence of titles – from *Airport 1975* to *Airport '77* and then *Airport '80— The Concorde*.

Coming full circle, titles are now becoming complicated all over again. About the only people who can be happy with this trend are the poets who for years have felt that they only existed to have their works plundered by novelists and playwrights and screenwriters in search of titles.

But enough of sequels. The films listed here all resorted to quotation for their titles. Where did they originate? The answers are on page 115.

1
Chariots of Fire

2
All the President's Men

3
Where Were You When the Lights Went Out?

Answers
Titles II

1

Blake, *Milton* (better known as 'Jerusalem'):
'Bring me my bow of burning gold
Bring me my arrows of desire
Bring me my spear! Oh, clouds, unfold
Bring me my chariot of fire.' (Note the singular. 'Chariots of
fire' occurs in 2 Kings 6:17.)

2

An allusion to the nursery rhyme 'All the King's Horses and
all the King's Men' and perhaps the book and film about
Huey Long *All the King's Men*. There is a closer link to the
Nixon presidency, however: Henry Kissinger was fond of
trying to close White House ranks at the time of the 1970
Cambodia invasion by saying: 'We are [all] the President's
men and we must behave accordingly.'

3

The film deals with the great New York blackout of 1965
when the electricity failed and the birth rate (according to
legend) went up nine months later. The title echoes an old
song or rhyme 'Where was Moses when the lights went out?
(Down in the cellar eating sauerkraut.')

4

Edward Albee found the title for his play/film as a
piece of graffiti, based in turn upon the title of a song
from Walt Disney's *Three Little Pigs*, 'Who's afraid of
the big bad wolf'.

5

From Second World War radio news bulletins
came the phrase 'From all these operations X of our
aircraft are missing.'

6

From the Pledge of Allegiance to the Flag (put into its final form by Francis Bellamy, 1892): 'I pledge allegiance to the flag of the United States of America and to the republic for which it stands, one nation under God, indivisible, with liberty and justice for all.'

7

From *The Book of Common Prayer*, 'Forms of Prayer to be Used at Sea': 'Be pleased to receive into thy Almighty and most gracious protection the persons of us thy servants, and the Fleet in which we serve.'

8

From *The Book of Common Prayer*, 'The Litany': 'From all the deceits of the world, the flesh, and the devil, Good Lord, deliver us.'

9

The Gospel According to St Mark 3:25: 'If a house be divided against itself, that house cannot stand.'

10

US Constitution, Senate Rule 38: 'The final question on every nomination shall be, "Will the Senate advise and consent to this nomination?" '

11

The Gospel According to St Matthew 6:9 (also Luke 11:2)

12

Proverbs 11:29: 'He that troubleth his own house shall inherit the wind.'

13

From a West Indian calypso, used as the title of a novel by Audrey Erskine Lindop.

14

Stephen Vincent Benét, *American Names*: 'I shall not rest quiet at Montparnasse . . . Bury my heart at Wounded Knee.'

15

Matthew Henry (1662–1714) Attrib.

16

Francis Thompson, *The Kingdom of God*: 'The angels keep their ancient places;
Turn but a stone and start a wing!
'Tis ye, 'tis your estranged faces,
That miss the many-splendoured thing.'

Rotten Tomatoes

A problem that afflicts people who mix with actors and musicians after a performance is what to say when compliments do not flow easily. The professional view is that in such a situation only compliments are appropriate. Criticism can wait till tomorrow. However, Max Beerbohm came up with the nicely equivocal 'My dear girl, good is not the word!' for one leading lady, and experimenters in this field should pay heed to Beatrice Lillie, who may or may not have meant well when she dashed into a colleague's dressing-room on a first night and said 'Darling, I don't care what *anybody* says – *I* thought you were marvellous.' The best way out is simply not to mix with the artistic. Rotten tomatoes may then squelch freely.

A great American need not fear the hand of his assassin; his real demise begins only when a friend like Mr Sorensen closes the mouth of his tomb with a stone.

> *Nigel Dennis, reviewing* Kennedy *by Theodore C. Sorensen*

If white bread could sing, it would sound like Olivia Newton-John.

> *Anon*

It's like *Parsifal* without the jokes.

> *Noël Coward on* Camelot

Funny, without being vulgar.

> *W. S. Gilbert on Beerbohm Tree's* Hamlet

No!

Hannen Swaffer on the revue Yes and No, *1938*

Oh, for an hour of Herod!

Anthony Hope on the first night of Barrie's play Peter Pan

Crossroads – the TV soap opera whose acting gives trees a bad name.

Tim Satchell, Daily Mail

Travels by Edward Heath is a reminder that Morning Cloud's skipper is no stranger to platitude and longitude.

Christopher Wordsworth, The Observer

Full steam ahead. Ho ho!

I'm Being A Handbag

Dame Edith Evans had been excluded from some improvisational exercises during a rehearsal at the Old Vic because it was thought she might not approve. In time, a peculiar noise emerged from where she was sitting in the auditorium. A voice inquired anxiously 'Dame Edith, what's the matter?' 'I'm being a handbag,' she replied.

Stories abound about this wonderful actress, who died in 1976.

When a young actor wished her luck before a radio broadcast, she said:
'With some of us it isn't luck.'

When a Fortnum and Mason salesgirl insisted on fetching her threepence change:
'Keep the change, my dear, I trod on a grape as I came in.'

When told that Kenneth Williams had been cast in a play with her:
'But why? He's got such an extraorrrrdinary vooooiiiiicccce.'

When asked by a young actress how to set about speaking her lines:
'Say everything as if it is improper.'

When in the midst of supposed rivalry with Sybil Thorndike:
'If I'm to have a new frock, I insist that Sybil has a new cardigan.'
and
'I don't know whether I like her or not, but I've named my new bicycle after her.'

When urging a young actress to get on with her scene:
'I'm a very old lady. I may die during one of your pauses.'

When shortly after being awarded the DBE, she was
addressed by a call-boy with the words,
'Ten Minutes, Miss Evans':
'*Miss* Evans? It'll be Edie next!'

<u>Fermez Les Guillemets!</u>

It is almost time to close the quotation marks. But first, here are some more concluding words from literary works. Where are they taken from? The answers are on page 124.

1
The whole world's in a terrible state o' chassis.

2
It is closing time in the gardens of the West and from now on an artist will be judged only by the resonance of his solitude or the quality of his despair.

3
C'est mon panache!

4
Now I stretch out my hand, and from the further shore I bid adieu to all who have cared to read any among the words that I have written.

5
Good God, people don't do such things.

6
And out again, upon the unplumb'd, salt, estranging sea.

7
The son of a bitch stole my watch.

8
I lingered around them, under that benign sky: watched the moths fluttering among the heath and hare-bells; listened to the soft wind breathing through the grass; and wondered how anyone could ever imagine unquiet slumbers for the sleepers in that quiet earth.

9
The best of men is only a man at best,
And a hare, as everyone knows, is only a hare.

10
'For me . . . there still remains the cocaine-bottle.' And he
stretched his long, white hand up for it.

11
So we beat on, boats against the current, borne back
ceaselessly into the past.

12
No wonder George Eliot's husband fell into
the Grand Canal.

Answers
<u>Fermez Les Guillemets!</u>

1

Sean O'Casey, *Juno and the Paycock*

2

Cyril Connolly, in the final issue of the literary magazine
Horizon, 1950

3

Edmund Rostand, *Cyrano de Bergerac*

4

Anthony Trollope, *Autobiography*
(published posthumously)

5

Henrik Ibsen, *Hedda Gabler*

6

John Fowles, *The French Lieutenant's Woman* (words
which occur also in 'To Marguerite – Continued' by
Matthew Arnold)

7

Charles MacArthur and Ben Hecht, *The Front Page*

8

Emily Brontë, *Wuthering Heights*

9

Kit Williams, *Masquerade*

10
Sir Arthur Conan Doyle, *The Sign of Four*

11
F. Scott Fitzgerald, *The Great Gatsby*

12
James Morris, *Venice*

Si Monumentum Requiris, Circumspice

Sir Christopher Wren's son composed the famous epitaph for his father in St Paul's Cathedral: 'If you seek for a monument, look around you'.

Others, too, have been rewarded by the choice of delightfully suitable inscriptions on their graves or memorials. 'He being dead, yet speaketh' is the apt and prophetic text on the grave of the Reverend Francis Kilvert at Bredwardine – chosen long before his posthumously published diaries became known.

John O'Hara, the American writer, rewarded himself with a self-justifying claim in Princeton cemetery: 'Better than anyone else, he told the truth about his time, the first half of the twentieth century. He was a professional. He wrote honestly and well.'

Poor Robert Louis Stevenson suffered the ultimate insult: his famous lines 'Home is the sailor/Home from sea' were misquoted on his gravestone.

To whom do the following epitaphs apply? One or two are not of actual people. One or two are in translation. The answers are on page 129.

1

Hic jacet ********, rex quondam rexque futurus.

2

In Affectionate Remembrance of ******* ******* . . . died at the Oval, on 29th August, 1882. Deeply lamented by a large circle of sorrowing friends and acquaintances.
R.I.P. N.B. – The body will be cremated, and the ashes taken to Australia.

3

His foe was folly and his weapon wit.

4

Here I await Heaven's vengeance upon a vile assassin.

5

A Poet, Naturalist, and Historian, who left scarcely
any style of writing untouched, and touched none that
he did not adorn.

6

Here lies one whose name was writ in water.

7

Free at last, free at last, thank God Almighty,
we are free at last.

8

To strive, to seek, to find, and not to yield.

9

Good friend, for Jesus sake forbeare
To digg the dust encloased heare.
Blese be ye man yt spares thes stones,
And curst be he yt moves my bones

10

Where savage indignation can tear his heart no more.

11

They buried him among the Kings because he had done
good toward God and toward his house.

12

Cast a cold Eye
On Life, on Death.
Horseman, pass by!

"

Answers
Si Monumentum Requiris, Circumspice

1

(Arthurus) Said to have been written on the tombstone of King Arthur according to Malory, *Le Morte d'Arthur*.

2

(English cricket) When an English team was beaten by Australia, *The Sporting Times* announced the 'death' in this fashion. The following year, when England won, some Melbourne ladies presented the team with real 'ashes' – of the stumps and bails.

3

Inscription on the memorial to Sir William S. Gilbert in Victoria Embankment Gardens, London, composed by Anthony Hope, 1915.

4

On the Commendatore's statue in Mozart's *Don Giovanni*.

5

(Translated from the Latin) Dr Johnson's epitaph for Oliver Goldsmith.

6

Keats's own epitaph to be found on the grave of the 'Young English Poet' in the English cemetery, Rome.

7

The words quoted by Martin Luther King in his 'I Have a Dream' speech, on his own grave in Atlanta.

8

Words from Tennyson's *Ulysses* chosen by Apsley Cherry-Garrard to be put on the cross erected in Antarctica to commemorate the deaths of Captain Scott and company on their return from the South Pole.

9

William Shakespeare's apt inscription (probably written by Bacon!) in Holy Trinity, Stratford-upon-Avon.

10

(Translated from the Latin) 'Swift sleeps under the greatest epitaph in history' (W. B. Yeats) in St Patrick's Cathedral, Dublin.

11

Based on 2 Chronicles 24:16 – part of the inscription on the tomb of the Unknown Warrior, Westminster Abbey.

12

In Drumcliff churchyard, Co. Sligo, near a mountain called Ben Bulben is the inscription penned by W. B. Yeats one year before his death in a poem called 'Under Bulben'.

Adding To The Gaiety Of Nations

When David Garrick died, his friend Samuel Johnson uttered a breath-taking panegyric. 'I am disappointed by that stroke of death,' he said, 'which has eclipsed the gaiety of nations, and impoverished the public stock of harmless pleasure.' At once, Boswell queried his use of the plural 'nations' and the tameness of 'harmless pleasure'. But Johnson defended his praise of Garrick.

Anthologising and re-anthologising the more remarkable inscriptions and memorials to be found in churches and graveyards is a venerable activity in jeopardy these days owing to the decline of the fashion for such things. Nevertheless, I believe the following epitaphs have not been recorded before. Far from impoverishing the public stock of harmless pleasure, they add to it.

The Lord hath need of him. Mark XI.iii.

> *Weston-super-Mare— the text refers to an ass*

Now with Christ which is far better.

> *Brompton cemetery, on grave of woman buried alongside her husband*

Rest in Peace
Until we meet again.

> *a loving wife in memory of her husband, Hindhead churchyard*

Sarah Fletcher, wife of Captain Fletcher, who died in 1799 at the age of 29 and whose artless beauty, innocence of mind and gentle manners, once obtained for her the love and esteem of all who knew her. But when nerves were too delicately spun to bear the rude shakes and jostlings which we meet in this transitory world, nature gave way. She sunk and died a martyr to excessive sensibility.

*Clifton Hampden
churchyard*

Here lies the body of Edmund Gray
Who died maintaining his right of way.
He was right – dead right – as he drove along,
But he's just as dead as if he'd been wrong.

*no doubt apocryphal,
twentieth century*

Deep in this grave lies lazy Dai,
Waiting the last great trump on high.
If he's fond of his grave as he's fond of his bed,
He'll be last man up when the roll call's said.

> *Nevern, translated from the Welsh*

Leg of an Italian sailor. 1898.

> *Jeddah, Saudi Arabia*

Left us in peace, Febry 2nd, 1910.

> *San Michele, Venice*

Sir Richard Rose, who died 20th April 1913 from the effects of an aeroplane flight.

> *Mapledurham church*

Major. Born a dog. Died a gentleman.

pet's grave

Down the lanes of memory
The lights are never dim
Until the stars forget to shine
We shall remember her.

In Memoriam column,
Lancashire newspaper

Safe in the arms of Jesus (inserted by her loving husband).

In Memoriam column,
Calcutta Statesman

We miss him in the morning
We miss him at evening too
But we miss him most on Sundays
Because we have less to do.

In Memoriam column,
Gloucester Citizen

Here lies W********* S**********. Died 14th May 1843.
All his life he loved sailors.

Sonning, Berkshire

In memory of Maggie who in her time kicked two colonels,
four majors, ten captains, twenty-four lieutenants,
forty-two sergeants, four hundred and thirty-two other
ranks, and one Mills bomb.

army mule's grave,
somewhere in France

In loving memory of my beloved wife, Hester, the mother of
Edward, Richard, Mary, Penelope, John, Henry, Michael,
Susan, Emily, Charlotte, Amelia, George, Hugh, Hester,
Christopher and Daniel. She was great breeder of pugs, a
devoted mother and a dear friend.

Hemel Hempstead

Always tidy neat and clean,
Lost his life in a submarine.

In Memoriam column,
Scottish newspaper

Index

Envoi

You have delighted us long enough.

Jane Austen, Pride and Prejudice

What They Said:

About Cannes

'Cannes is where you lie on the beach and stare at the stars or vice versa'

About Cambridge

'For Cambridge people rarely smile
Being urban, squat, and packed with guile'

About Zaire

'The people of Zaire are not thieves.
It merely happens that they move things, or borrow them'

About New York

'It's not Mecca. It just smells like it'